Melodies of the Broken Reed

Heartaches and Headaches—A Poetic Healing

With profound love & regards
to dear
Brother Sudarshan Sehgal
Bhabi Erika Sehgal
from —
R.B. Bhandari
7·3·09

Melodies of the Broken Reed

Heartaches and Headaches—A Poetic Healing

R K Bhushan

AUTHORSPRESS

Worldwide Circulation through Authorspress Global Network
First Published 2009
by
Authorspress
E-35/103, Jawahar Park
Laxmi Nagar, Delhi-110 092
e-mail: authorspress@yahoo.com

Melodies of the Broken Reed:Heartaches and Headaches—A Poetic Healing
ISBN 978-81-7273-481-7

Printed in India at Tarun Offset, Delhi.

Dedicated

With total reverence, obeisance and surrender

To

SAI BABA

Whose Eternal Presence Works

To

Enlighten the Course of Life Here and Everywhere

and

Whose Infinite Grace

is cleansing my inner being

for a life in His Creation.

Preface

Heartaches and headaches are invariably and indispensably interwoven in the grand pattern of everybody's life since the time of creation. Increasing awareness of our ignorance of life's infinity, with all the marvels of advancement and expansion, and infinitely greater infinite grace of the Almighty influence the course of our life. Thus is born the process of creation. Creative spirit runs and works in every being, every moment, everywhere. Otherwise the process of eternal evolution will not fulfil and accomplish the Master's vision.

Songs in this book are the product of personal pains and passions, experienced in that eternal process of evolution, though their outburst became irresistible at different times. The songs are also born out my living concern for human caring and sharing. It only strengthened my conviction that humans must work and live for mutual love and happiness. This substance will mould, carve and shape the images and illustrations of the Divine, re-writing the future history of man, and re-defining his role and place in the cosmos. The bleeding and stinking pages of the ages of human history will then appear to be all falsehood uttered to portray man as a cannibal.

I am sure that the process has already started. I am sure that our progeny will bless us in their bliss. These songs silently sing what I have felt, seen and what I envision. Poetry is never a statement or an opinion made or expressed by an individual. It is a sudden and spontaneous bursting of the lament or cry or moan of the heart wounded and bleeding in the shadows of the enlightened soul. Or it is a song of the joy of immensity felt at the warmth and light of love that blooms into a smile on the mouth or a glow on the face of the poor lover. The dust of time has dried the bleeding but its layer has veiled the wounds. Now unseen, because lost, in the smiles on the mouth.

Presented with love to the feeling heart and thinking head! Cheers!

R.K.Bhushan

Acknowledgements

I am especially grateful to Sudarshan Kcherry for a variety of reasons. I may not state them all. But I must say that I met him only once in Delhi; that too for three hours in March 2008. We fixed our meeting in a South Delhi restaurant. Without knowing any mark or sign of his identity, I headed for the appointed place. I was astonished when he greeted me on my reaching there with a warm, broad smile and led me where we were to sit and chat, and we were comfortable and enthusiastic about whatever we embarked on. Even the service staff served and listened to us graciously.

I didn't know about him. But I felt as if I were watching an all-absorbing movie for the first time in life or I was drinking with a man who was unfolding and revealing to me what I had never concealed and what I was showing to him also. In such a situation, neither of us had a feeling of sanity and we parted saying unforgettable byes on the traffic-deluged roads of South Delhi that late evening.

Sudarshan Kcherry, I am happy to address him informally, is a well-meaning personality. We share much in common at the ideological level. We have long talks frequently on serious issues that confront man and mankind and do feel that something concrete must be done to create conditions of clean and zestful life on this planet to embrace one day the cosmic glory. We realise that the environment needs to be awakened to liberate life from the stench of goons, loons and toons.

Also I feel proud of my children—Sheenam, Geetika and Vishal Sabharwal—who have shown the worth of their strong and honest character and personality in the face of the odds of daily life. This attitude of theirs has strengthened further my own faith in the goodness of life blessed by the Infinity, SAI BABA. I am confident that the struggle of their blooming, golden youth is a sure sign of their rich harvest of the splendid virtues of life in the very near future.

Now I leave it to Sudarshan Kcherry who has attained antiquity in such a short time to bring out this book in a way that graces his friendship and personality.

R.K.Bhushan

Contents

1. Glow and Glory of the Divine

Glowing colours rained in my bosom
When I saw you first.
Dance of breezes then
Brought in my soul
A shower,
A spectrum,
Celestial glow,
A riot of colours.
All merged into the rhythmic melody
Of love pure and beauty sure.
What moments
Amidst the trash of existence!
Bliss is beauty and beauty is bliss
With truth that is lost in synthesis.

Muse doesn't amuse;
Olympus has crashed
Into fragments of frozen love;
Petals are born withered,
Flowers blown blow no freshness;
The wrinkled earth
Is fretted
With arson and armour;
The majesty of the mountains,
The splendour of meadows,
The denuded woods weep;
The thunderous message of rocks
Is silenced
In the mighty explosion of dynamite.

Ages hence,
The archeologists,
Will piece together
The story of civilisation
To be recited by the curates!

SAI ?
You are the seer-of-all and see all,
You are the knower-of-all and know all,
You are the doer-of-all and do all,
In forms and spirits
Infinite and infinite spaces
To sanctify total existence,
Yesterday, today and tomorrow —
All is your domain.

Your integrated vision
Is disintegrated
Into isms and creeds,
And sects select
With faiths multifacet.
This assures and gives
Loaves and fishes
Of luxuries and riches;
Sentiments are fired
Goons are hired.
Toons work and loons shirk.

So you watch gleefully
This evolution
To create certainty and sanctity
Of Man in Eternity?
Your vision of Infinity
Your creation fulfilling
In form and formlessness
And forms endless?
Perhaps you need not answer.
A little awareness of the Supreme
Makes it all self-explanatory,
Although darker regions dominate
To delude and delay
And also deny
The ultimate destiny and destination.
It saddens you not?
Your work goes on
With greater cheer!

2. The Unsaid

Left to my loneliness,
With endless crowds of memories,
The present haunts me.
Desertion and isolation
Alone seem true today.
Long back,
Amidst cheering crowds,
Life was not a hoax.
Now it is a waste
Of all my pursuit
Of ideals and wisdom
Which lies scattered all around.

Now stares and mocks at me
Ruins of love and learning,
Ruins of relations,
With none to care and comfort.
It is a sight of dreams
Undone.
And hopes shattered.
Sleep has become a stranger.
So no dreams of future.
Only a thought of dark end solaces!
Visions are blurred and bleared
With bleak and dismal days.
A little gap in the lips
Makes passage
For deep heavy sighs —

From the ashes and sparks
Of smouldering bosom!
All that man is,
Wrapped in grandeur
Of beauty and light,

3

Tells the tale
Of destiny —
Destiny that he builds
And Destiny that governs him.
Destiny built is as ordained.
So is the other one.
The strings of life
Keep producing sounds
Of the song sung eternally!
With the touch of whose fingers
We know not!

3. The Chosen Fate

Dreaming of
The beauty, romance and love
Of princesses and princes
While living among
The common and the commonest,
Aware of their looks,
Disgusting and freakish,
With no sense of intellectual beauty
And no vision afar,
Dead to all dreams,
I sowed the seeds of tragedy.
Still doing all that could be done
To lift them.
Quite late came the realisation
Common mean vices
Gripped them always
Trapping my dreams
In their plottings
Mocking my love
And concealing their delight
In my soulful of agonies.

Whirling emotions
In the eddies of love
Raised qualms of conscience.
Looking to eternity for fulfilment,
This poor brief man
Wasted himself in sighs and yearnings.
Be the earthiest of the earthy
In love, lore and leanings
To avoid pain and misery.

4. Living With the Pangs of Partition

Bharata, Burma or Bengal,
All is our hoary past—
The glory of our shared history,
Religion, culture and customs.
We have divided—
Our houses and havelis,
Our families and fields,
Our parents and progeny
And our daughters and their dowries!
Our states and estates
Stood scattered
In divisions, sub-divisions
And fragmentations.
Narrow dark alleys
And zig-zag lanes
Amidst our ancestral dwellings—
Contours of our celebrated geography!

All speak proudly
Of our intents and purposes
Since times afar—
No explanation and justification needed—
Mapping the labyrinths
Of our disgraced history,
Of our surrender and servitude
To invaders and traders,
Innumerable!
Today we chant,
Bravely and proudly,
Mera Bharata Mahaan!

1947 Partition is a subject fertile
With scholars and students alike.

Both are at pains
To achieve personal expansion
And academic growth.
They neither know nor feel
Pains and pangs, rapes and ravages,

Shame and disgrace,
Terror and trauma,
Of the gashes gaping
And wounds aching
With blood congealed
With the dust of Time
Over them.

Exodus largest!
The procession of strangers,
Stunned and benumbed,
Drowned in doings of destiny,
History leads through lands
Known and unknown,
With agonizing burdens and pains
Into the future blank,
Even today!

The darkest-ever tragedy
In human history,
Though its living witnesses
And their evidence of future
Have thrived and reached summits.
Still they express their aspirations strong
In People-to-People contact
And the like
To revisit the lands
Of their roots and clans
To be re-united!

We were divided
Among the British, the French
And the Portuguese.

And among ourselves!
So are we today
With all our regional imbalances!
Sharpening the edges of history
Our hates and intolerance
Are stronger than before.
Larger fears and terrors
Suppress our sense of revolt.

And the lines of division
Continue to be drawn
At bottom.

Thanks that
The sun, the skies, the stars and the spaces
Are still beyond us!
Perhaps divided we stand
And united we fall—
Chosen fate of us all !

5. Show of the Shadows

Shadows show
The shadowy show.

Shadows we are,
Shadows we remain,
Shadows we seek,
Shadows we chase,
Shadows we see,
Shadows we gain.
Shadows merge into shadows,
Shadows emerge out of shadows.

Shadows also have a form;
Shadows inhabit the holy land
And strive to make it waste land.

Our faith,
Our religious teachers and guides,
Our sages and the essence of our lives,
Awaken us
To the shadows—
That people our world
To appease us,
To please us, to fleece us,
To tease us
And to squeeze us at last!

Shadows shape us.
Shadows shape our life.
Shadows shape our destiny.
Shadows begin to shrink
When we are on the brink
Dreaming of shadows
That stalk and sink

Into the fathomless perilous seas
Leaving behind
History of shadows
Playing with the present
To define future!
Quest for the Truth,
Search for the reality,
Whatever it be—
We play with the shadows!

6. The Delicate Fabric

The Wheel of Fate,
The Wheel of Destiny,
The Wheel of Time —
All are running the mill of life.
Their stones
Are grinding, gruelling and grilling
The substance
Of human strife, sweat and dreams
To fulfil ambitions and aspirations
Of everybody and everywhere.
None and nothing can stop it.
Also all that
Nature yields and adores,
To comfort man
For relief and reward.

Thus goes on the process
Of moulding, carving and shaping
The fabric of Life.
Ceaselessly!
Countless hands work simultaneously,
Day and night,
On the sea, sky and earth.
Even when
The creations crash, crumble and collapse,
The work continues
Amidst fret, fever and fun.
And there is no hegemony,
No hybridisation;
No pastiche, nothing amorphous.
Only the imperfection
Of sight and sense feels so.

7. Cheers!

My soul skylarked
Amidst singing birds,
Blooming plants,
And blossoming trees
Where the restlessly playful
Multi-hued butterflies
And the soothing morning breeze
Stormed the citadels of sunlight
In my ever-fresh little garden.
It was the harmony of heaven.
It blessed me with the wealth
No amount of life's labour,
In human world could ever give.

The cooling balm made me oblivious,
Of the injuries and the bleeding wounds.
These moments of light and delight
Sang a lullaby
And lulled me to sleep
From which I didn't want to wake.

But wake I must
Lest life's purpose should be lost!

8. Light, Light, and Light !

Lamp that lights the world,
Lamp that we light —
Both light us not
But only show
What interests us not
And what interests us most!

Debris of the heart
Could crush me not;
Rubies of the head
Alone brushed the rot.
Balance between the rubies and the rot,
Again favoured the rubies.
It scared the Satanic thoughts.

9. The Divine Mantra

Rulers and leaders really tense;
Can't sleep, the poor noble souls!
Contemplating means
To nation's prosperity.
They come up with innovative ideas
That the twinkle of an eye
Convert men and matter into gold.
So they speak
Goldenly... of....?
And promise and plan
To move heaven and earth
To lead the nation to the top.
Which top? Sky is the limit!
No poor or poverty
Will inhabit
This glorious land of ancient
GOLDEN SPARROW!

Billions of acres of our land
Lie unused,
Since ages.
They are suddenly aware!
What an awareness!
So every inch of land
Must fill empty state pockets
And enrich mafia coffers!

Divine Mantra of opulence!!
Labour pains of our new prophets?
Snakes of the deserts?
How true that desert snakes
Are more venomous and deadly!

10. The Promise of Nature

Fresh waters gushing forth
From the springs eternal
Fed the roots
Along the entire route
For ages
Through the woods and brooks.

Springs have gone dry
Leaving only the traces
Of their eternal flow.
Roots have withered
Or are dead.
Trees are denuded
Or dying.

Even rains are rare.
They do not engender virtue.
Deserts
Distinguish and adore
Life in life!
Idlers are idolises,
Idols are idle,
Ideals starve
And stray
Into alien territory!

To be prosecuted
And executed.

Lord of Life watches this
And this also—
Life's real riches robbed,
Treasures plundered,

Sinners flourish—
Sinners in society,
Sinners in saintly garb
Under
The patronage and protection
Of impotent will and toothless law.

I am still rooted in roots
And feel the rot
And am rotting.
Will you stem the rot, O Lord?

Is it evolution
Of new civilisation
Emerging from the Divine Dream
Of moulding, carving and shaping?

Perhaps so.
A comfort in rotting!

11. A Heap of Broken Glass

I looked around
And saw scattered
Countless pieces of glass,
Big and small—
Red, blue and green,
Yellow, white and maroon—
Plain but mostly stained.
I swept them into a heap,
For they were all my past,
Daily dreams of days afar.

Rosy and royal,
Opulent and illuminating,
Promising peace and purity,
And tranquil felicity.
Happy reminders
Of the colours and stuff
The Creator chose and used
To weave and present
The pattern
Of beauty and bond.
We humans invariably are!

12. Tree

I wish
I were a tree
That never withholds
Its shade and fruit
From those
Who hurt and hit it.

It weathers
All storms
That give it
Sounding slaps
To take away
Its blossoms and fruits
In their infancy, prime and youth.

It stands
In all its peace and poise,
Majesty and magnanimity,
Without a frown,
Like the Lord of Happiness.
And smiles
At the hurting kids
And slapping storms,
Ruffling rains
And sustaining sun!

The world belongs
Not to the tree
But to its user friends.

And
The winning world
Goes!
Loveless
And Lifeless!

13. To a Friend

Dear Friend,
You are sun-down
And unwell!

I wonder!

Sun sustains life.
Nature, animal and human!
And all its beauty, balance and blessings,
And arts.
And it destroys
The enemies that ails life.

So why should it ail you?

You have been helping sun
To fulfil its fruitful fun
In all that you do.

Then why should you be
Sun-down?

Is sun annoyed
That
You are excelling Him?

14. The Message of Silence

The flowers
Give their message
In silence —
With their rich, soft
Bloom, colour and fragrance.

The star-studded skies
Convey their message
In silence
With their heavenly
Love, light and peace.

The stones
Give their message
In silence
With their grace,
Majesty and magnanimity.

The ancient mountains
Convey their message
In silence —
With their snow-caps and grassy laps —
Their melting dance and musing trance.

The moon-lit night
Conveys its message
In silence
With silky sails in earthy vales
Slimming into sanguine silvery dawn.

The sun
Conveys its message
In silence
With its riotous journey
Of colours cool, bright and gay.

Then, Dear, why
Is your silence alone
So intriguing?

15. Cracking the Code of Happines

I spared not myself
To spear through
The rocky roads
And cobbled paths
To plough my way
To happiness.

When sun scorched me not,
Thunder threatened me not,
Rain ruffled me not,
Storms stopped me not,
My quest led me on
To harvest rich.

Nature enlightened me
When I richly relished nature.
All sadness took to wings
And left me light
In mood and spirit
When the orchestral
Melodies of Nature
Melted into the magic rush
Of harmonious bliss.

Nature was ever-ready
To roll the treasures
Of beauty and wealth
When I chose,
With a smile,
Her lore and light.

16. Irony

The most astounding irony,
The irony of ironies
Of which we are aware
And also unaware
Is —
Our thought of death
Is dead;
Our will to live
Is feeble.
We are living in death,
We are dying to live.

Our coloured appearances
Glitter.
Glitter dazzles glitter
To resolve the paradox.

Our obsession for ostentation
Among the glitterati
Has caused a glitch
In life's sacred plan;
And relations fritter away.

Spirit smoulders,
Soul is half-dead,
Faith is fleshy
And flashy,
Truth is enmeshed
And badly bruised
In crooked meaning
Hooked to heady purpose!

We sustain healthy life?

We all know this
And delight in defeat.
Such turns and twists
Help us seek
Out-of-turn gains.

And life is not out of tune!

17. A Tale of Dreams

We are the shadows
Passing
In the naked nooks of night
Looking for a ray of light.

We walk on the earth
With eyes on the stars.
Skies swim and our eyes brim.

Our love-lulled hearts
And desire-dulled heads
Lead us to the pathways
Where we attempt in vain
To declare and establish
Our sovereignty.

The real fight begins;
Light grows dim;
Knowledge glows dark.
Fight lasts till
The last flicker
Puts it all out.

Look to the pathways,
Love and idolise them.
Think not of the stars—
Better to live and die
Larking with beauties here.
Living thus will take away
All cares and regrets.
When dead—
Out of ashes will emerge
Sparks as stars
To adore the strings of skies.

18. Heart's Treasures

My heart
Is a treasure house
Of pains —
Less of mine,
Largely of others.
So it aches not
And feels at ease,
With whatever is;
It prays with soul
To God
For what is not.

Whatever we beg from God,
He gives not alms
But blessings with grace.
Seek not from the beggars
But from the Donor
For the beggars can't be charitable.

Giving others relief,
Whatever be my endurance,
Has always made me happy;
It made many, many...
Envious.
Why should anyone share my happiness?
No alchemy or philosopher's stone
Could convert them into gold,
What iron they were!
Age-old universal wisdom
Can't be wrong.

19. Rough and Tumble Tragedy

The world where
Flatterers and fixers
Flourish and flutter;
The world where
Insecurity inspires them to be repressive;
The world where
The loss of advantage
Is relished by plebians.

Those who are to put out fires,
Dole out the standing promise
Of silent, stifled strategies
Authenticating submission
To suppression and slavery.

The din of dignity and respect
For human rights and freedoms
From fear and fratricide
Often submerges
In the deafening explosions.

Brutal expansionism
And democratic imperialism
Have changed
Their face and garb;
Of course, BENIGN!
And MAGNANIMOUS!

I watch the scenic beauty
Pitying myself as a prey
To prayers!
Hope is too true and committed
To desert!

20. Honour Killing?

Honour killing —
Rage of the time —
Adores the pages of the papers
Daily —
It is done out of rage.
With a sense of pride!
Hence savagery!
So where is the civilisation?

But what puzzles me is
If it is killing for honour
Or it is killing honour
Or saving honour by killing honour
Or it is honour to kill.
Does honour remain after killing?
Or it attains sanctity after killing?

Yes it does.
For honour for which
We live and die
And assert murderous safety
For it,
We know,
Is honour dishonoured,
Disfigured, disgraced or denied.

Of course, we are great in honour!

21. Agony of Burden

Agony of burden or burden of agony,
I don't know.
My sins seem heavier than virtues.
Otherwise why should I be sad and suffering?
Ever God-fearing, never man-fearing,
Always an ordinary human —
Never claimed to be an angel,
Never wanted to be a devil,
I did all that I could
To perfect my humanity —
To a rare default:
That was extremism,
The world doesn't accept.

What I said was jeered at;
What I did was leered at.

I should have been man-fearing —
To a pretence.

Vision, clear and higher,
With no thought
Of partial fulfillment,
Looking to God,
With hands raised,
To help me.
Help He did
But it didn't help
The vision.

Perhaps
My sight was defective,
My near vision was bad
That I couldn't see around.

Now the sight is sharper
And will for fulfilment
Has faded into obscurity
The past,
All looks a prelude
To the present
Quintessential!
God bless again!

22. Happiness

You are no more!
Do you think
I am anymore?

Both are not mistaken.
Still a mistake is there.

Whatever we are,
Wherever we are,
Let's be happy.

If we don't,
We'll ruin each other.

23. Paradox

I loved peace and order
But I found myself
Amidst conflict and disorder.

Mystery ignoble it remained.

I never wanted or aspired
For what they were hungry
'And even wolfish.
Fear-stricken,
They intrigued and conspired.

And their wolfishness
Reached sky-high.
So were my pleasure,
Peace and plenty.
Only God is to be thanked!

24. Seeking Your Mercy

Divine Mercy, Sai,
Has ever been your infinite
Wealth and Blessing.
And your kingdom has ever
Prospered and expanded
In temporal and celestial regions
And you have always been
Magnanimous
In showering them
On your devotees
Visiting your shrine
Or devoutly seeking refuge
At your abode, they say.

Your devotees,
In millions,
Day in and day out,
Have been singing
And reciting
Hymns and litanies
To praise you,
To adore you,
To idolise you,
Since you assumed human form,
To lead them
Into the world
Of bliss and beauty
And liberate them
From the suppressive suffering,
Misery and wretchedness.
Even after you returned
To your original Home,
You have been taking
Full care

Of your devotees
Looking to you.

I have never visited
Your shrine;
I have never recited
Or sung to you;
I have never adored
Or idolised you —
Ceremoniously!
And with the devotion
Of regularity!
Your devotees
Do inspire me
With the splendour and glory
Of your spirit, soul and supremacy.
And I also begin
To look to you and seek
Refuge at your feet
For your infinite grace
That may comfort me
And free my life from
Unsavoury and nasty times.

Do you listen, O beloved Sai?
And will you come to my relief?

25. Seeking Divine Mercy-2

I have sinned, am sinning
And can't help sinning.
If I don't,
I shall breed illusions
And rival you
Or try to rival you.
So let me be a sinner,
Aware and awake,
The finest comfort
In being a human.

My sins are for personal pleasure
Not to harm anyone;
Instead I seek
God's grace and blessings
For all
That they feel happy
In the happiness of all.

Then what
Sickening and debased feeling
Shall afflict mankind?

It is there and getting
Where it is not.
And shall become
The supreme
Reigning, raining, reining
Passion!

26. Ambition Belied

The seeds of Macbeth's
Noble destruction
Were scattered by
The Three Witches —
Masters of their Domain of Dread.
The Fourth
And Super Witch —
Royal Enchantress of the Surging Sea —
Led him on
To a head-on
Collision and bloody collapse
Making him immortal
In the corridors
Of Imperiality and regency
With blue blood frozen
And the purple red blood
Still oozing, dripping
And spreading across
The royal carpet
Of the glowing golden literature
And its critical concepts
Redefined!

I was neither born nor lived
Macbeth,
Nor was destined to be so,
Nor ever wanted to be so.
But Four witches
From the Domain of Delight
In Darkness and Debasement
Hounded me to degradation,
Though their vaulting ambition

To drag me to doom
Hit them all back
To reveal their revolting face!

The world has its own eyes
To view the victor and the vanquished!

27. Love Black and White

Desdemona was gullible;
So was Othello!
Iago gulled them into gullibility.

White and black merged;
On the paths
That remained rough,
Cobbled and thorny,
But created no new shades,
Though such merger creates grey.
Grey has many shades.
How great
That even today
The White and Black
Retain and sustain
Their full-blooded
And blooming identity!

And how true, honest and committed
In creating
Tempestuous black currents
From the fathomless Atlantic
To the ecstasy of Iago
Till the snows of Alabaster
Were splashed with black blood
In the dancing candle flame
To the murmurous tremulous sound
Of the wound
Of the angelic innocence
Of destiny de mona!

28. Those Moments ...

Those moments
Are lost
In their ever-fresh presence
When I held your hands,
And felt the crushing warmth;
Held you in my arms
And experienced the silken bliss;
Hugging you hard
Was a heaven of heavens!

Since those moments,
Life seems easy
Rich with tranquillity.
But lava erupting
Inside
Always tears me apart.
Sounds and lights,
Unheard and unseen
By you and all
Turns a living mirage!

29. Loss of Mourning

Times are ripe
For our—
Inability to mourn,
Refusal to mourn,
Formality to mourn.

Silence of the dead,
Silence of the living—
Alone clash
To deafen and deaden
The rhythm of the WORD.

The mourners seem broken
Or at least sad
And sympathetic;
Somewhat happy.
A variety of emotions
Surges and stares
On the saddened
Faces of mourners.

The family can't help mourning
And must do so
In all solemnity—
At least
Till the disposal of the dead.

The dead is awake
To the shattered illusion
Of living
To die for the dear ones.
And the pain subsides
In comfort of death

And peace that passes
All bliss.

Blame none.
The dead had to go
And the living must mourn
And live dying
For the trash
And riff-raff
Of relations and love
That defy truth
And feels solace in show!

30. A Tribute to a Class

All dunces danced in delight.
It was the day of the duds;
And he was born.
Since then, he has a virgin head,
Empty soul, cold heart and morals dead.
Blessed with the supremacy of senseless,
Decorated with the doctorate in dullness.
Recognized well in the land of crime,
Elsewhere he chooses to play mime.
The master saw glory in his noble vision,
Trusted him to guide higher education.
Language is dead, history is fled,
Philosophy is starved, politics is dwarfed.
Wisdom is dark, folly is bright,
Tensions of such blessed souls are light.
His mists rule and he is misty in rules,
His caucus fools and he is fisty with mules.
Stories of swains were his sole delight,
Wrestling with the wits gaily in his flight.
Boasting of high links was his hobby,
The dark and the denuded were his lobby.
Blessed fully in the exit of his shit,
Care of the belly with loose tongue was his only outfit.
Tall arrogant gay gait determined his fate,
Opium thrice a day was his soul mate.
He will stoop or escape when challenged,
It was the sure way to keep himself balanced.
Declarations high and pronouncements wise,
Only the members of his clan could surmise.
"Honour and shame from no question rise,
Play well thy part, there all the honour lies —"
Was his chief faith and scriptural rite,
Always for them, he gave sacred fight.
The real gem of meankind,
To light he was totally blind.

31. The Vision Beatific

The Knower of secrets
Buried fathomless in bosoms,
The Knower of every heartbeat
That symbolizes life —
He walks
And the earth dances in rhythm;
He moves with compassion infinite
For the simple and the simpleton,
For the swain and the slain,
For the smart and the sagacious.
He cares and caresses and comforts
The wounded and the sick and the broken.

The Embodiment of Truth,
The Personification of Love,
The Advent of Light,
The Flame of Fire Bright,
Performing the Divine Miracles
In the manifestations rich
And the pageant and the panorama
Is bewitched-least knowing
The Presence of the Master!

His sermons and songs,
His Dance and Drama —
All His Performing Arts —
Bathed and Enlightened
In the glorious simplicity
And sublime comedy —
Are directed to destroy
The darkness
Of and amidst
His devout devotees!

Seeing in His shows
The planetary ascension
To The Ultimate,
Age after age,

Unending
And without a beginning,
Is the mystery
Of your enchanting tricks,
Unfolding the blooming beauties

Of your Domain
To entrance your creation!
HE is The SAI
Who defines and underlines
The countless hues and shades
Of the meaning and purpose
Of moving, existing and living.

But the poor we,
Are dull or slow
To see and realize
His Eternal Consciousness
In the ever-advancing,
Ever-expanding evolution,
Ever guiding, ever-supervising
Life marching
Through His Performing Arts,
To rectify our misdeeds!
This SAI NATH!

32. Sai Saar

Another day gone waste,
SAI wants me to haste
To retreat
To the paths He enkindles
For cosmic perfection.
SAI says—
No riddles, no puzzles!
He says—
Similes simple
And metaphors mellifluous;
He recites and narrates,
Directly and frankly,
Easy means to achieve
The most difficult—
The Cosmic Domain
Unfurling and rolling
The golden and the green
With white sheen.

He says—
No double speak,
No double talk.
The present is haunted
By the shadows of the past.
Our harvest is what we have sown;
So we see what we show;
We receive what we give;
We listen what we say.
Our focus is selfish cares
Where our dross glares.

SAI says—
Our mind's mirror
Is smoked, soiled and smeared

With layers of sin and vice;
We live a life of lies
And assert them
For gains to be a glitterati.
It wrongs us
Into happiness elusive.
We knowingly choose
To build a heaven of tensions
And belie our instinctive reclensions.
We look the other way
To remedy our apprehensions.
We consciously cheat
None but ourselves

And dig the grave of happiness.
We scatter the stink
And bemuse and flog
The weaklings on the brink.

SAI says—
Ego is ruinous
To total happiness;
It darkens the glow
Of the Divine Domain.
So touch softly the strings
And sing the strain of life
With compassion that brings
What the Master of All,
The Absolute and Tall,
The Ultimate and the Scroll,
Dreams for the future Call.

So stem the floods
Of your sufferings and miseries,
Check the deluge
Of your pain and agony;
End the hell
Of your troubles.
How?

I tell you—
Demolish the confines of your self,
Sacrifice for the good of others,
Deny not the Truth,
Dry not your Faith,
Be not cowardly to be good,
Be bold to be bad,
Fear not hearsay,
Dare to fight injustice,
Tyranny and suppression,
Love others' happiness
As your own—
This is the ethics,
This is the religion and the righteous,
All else is unethical and irreligious!
Let it happen
And see Heaven
Where dwells One—
The Master of All!